For dad

Delicious Pieces of Home
By Jyoti Patel

One mouthful takes you back to a thousand moments already lived. Your body stays here, in London, but your mind is in Lahore. The sound of your mother preparing a pot of aloo gosht, humming quietly to herself, the clinking of steel pans being nudged slightly to make room for one more, the scent of coriander and cumin and turmeric twirling around her. Her movements are a dance: the slicing, the stirring, the sprinkling of spice. Each dish choreographed.

You are there with her, your bare feet cool against the floor, muscle memory leading you along the same routine of slicing, stirring, sprinkling. Outside the fading green doors, the rush of the bustling market, children playing cricket, scooters weaving merrily between them, a young woman capturing it all on film. A camera clicking, a sheet of black thrown over the front of your home. You pause, trying to figure out if this has already happened, or if it is something yet to come, decades away, something that's waiting for you.

Before you can decide, the kitchen timer cuts you short. Its ring echoes backwards, blurring this moment into another. You do not know which came first, in what order they belong, but you know they are memories and that they are yours. Yesterday or tomorrow, it is your father's turn in the kitchen. A special occasion. The rich, creamy warmth of nargisi kofta on your tongue. Under it, a whisper of something else—cardamom and sugar and ghee. Gulab jamun from the shop down the alley. Oily and sweet. Saved for later.

The scent of it leads you further, to a trail of your future, which is also your past. A kitchen of your own one day, named after your mother. On the walls, sixteen squares of paper. Recipes. Memories. It doesn't matter which because there is little difference between the two in a world where recipes are passed like stories, words carried in the air. These squares of paper are your attempts to immortalise scents, home, memories, all things transient. *Murgh makhani. Chana palak. Khichri. The rice is on the hob. The dog's in the car. Don't forget your teeth, dad.* That last one makes you laugh but you're unsure why. A flash of a shop floor, a smile made only of gums. A snippet of your future, one you haven't lived through but still your belly aches from the memory of the laughter that is yet to leave your lips.

You carry the squares of paper with you because to carry them is to carry home. Your daughter will one day sit inside of these memories, wondering how she can feel so at home in a place she can't even remember being in. *The initials of two brothers scratched into wood. The call of a parrot, charming you for sweets. Cutlets with peas after school. Looking up to a perfect rectangle of sky. Eggs and bread in Hounslow. A tower made of charity shop caps.* You wonder—are these recipes or are they memories or are they love? Is there truly a difference? You will carry them across oceans, these pieces, handing them down to your children, your children handing them back to you as their own iteration of love, such as that which you hold in your hands as you read this, as you savour these delicious pieces of home.

My mum used to make simpler versions of Pakoras, these were usually just Potatoes and onions dipped in batter with a tamarind sauce for tea time with chai. We'd eat the pakoras on the floor of my parents' bedroom with cushions. My family would often eat them to break fast during Ramadan.

SERFRAZ PAKORAS (VG, GF)

A family favourite, these filling fritters are often sold at street vendors in Lahore. Crispy on the outside, with a tender-soft inside, they are a perfect starter or snack.

Serves 4-6 (makes 20 pakoras)

1 medium brown onion
julienned
2 medium potatoes
peeled and finely chopped
50g spinach
washed and finely chopped
¼ white cabbage
finely chopped
1-2 green chillies
finely chopped
1 tsp chilli powder
½ tsp Kashmiri chilli powder
¼ tsp ground turmeric
½ tsp salt
500g gram flour
125g self-raising flour
½tsp baking soda
250ml water
500ml sunflower or vegetable oil
10g of fresh coriander
finely chopped

optional for colouring, not spice

1. Place the onion, potatoes, spinach, cabbage, spices, salt and fresh coriander into a bowl.

2. Add your gram flour, self-raising flour and baking soda, combining all of the ingredients with your hands.

3. Add the water little by little, while continuing to mix with your hands until you reach a thick and sticky consistency. If the mixture is too runny, add more gram flour slowly and mix well; if too thick add more water slowly.

4. Set aside the mixture in the fridge for at least 30 minutes.

5. Using a wok or deep pan, heat the oil over a medium-high flame. When you think it is hot enough, test by adding a spoonful of the mixture—it is ready if it floats to the top of the oil.

6. Use a large tablespoon to drop the mixture into the oil and cook in batches of 5-6 at a time. Keep flipping the pakoras until they darken and turn crispy. This should take about 5 minutes.

7. Once cooked, transfer into a bowl lined with kitchen towel to soak up the excess oil.

8. Enjoy with my mint, mango and tamarind sauce.

or Ketchup!

Tonys top ten spices!

- Chilli powder
- Curry powder
- Coriander seeds
- Yellow poppy seeds
- Sesame seeds
- Cumin seeds
- Black onion seeds
- Garam masala
- Cumin powder
- Turmeric

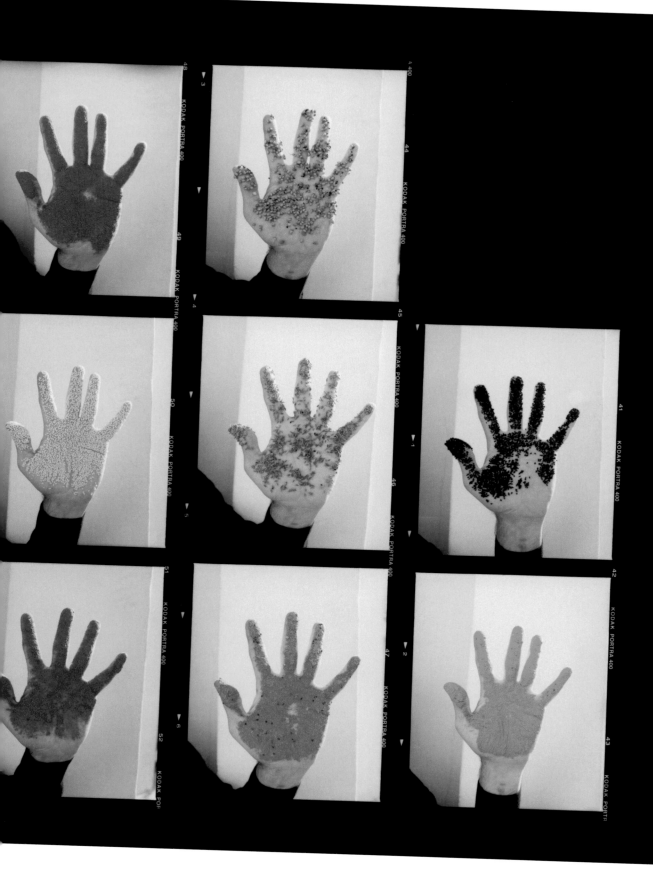

What is your favourite dish, and who cooks it the best?

Aloo Gosht by mum + dad.

"Pakoras with tamarind, mint and mango sauce, made by dad."

This was my dad's special I'd eat them at occasions such as weddings or large
Parties. The dish is very good looking, but easy to make lots of. People are always
impressed by Nargisi Koftas.

NARGISI KOFTA (GF)

Hard-boiled eggs encased in spicy minced meat, among a rich sauce and potatoes. A favourite of the Mughals and named after the Narcissus flower, this is an impressive yet simple-to-make dish.

2 large brown onions
  finely sliced
750g lean beef or mutton mince
1½ tsp coriander powder
2 tsp chilli powder
½ tsp Kashmiri chilli powder
1½ tsp ground cumin
1 tsp garam masala
4 whole cloves
½ tsp ground turmeric
1 tsp salt
¼ tsp ground black pepper
2 tbsp gram flour
1 tsp butter
30g fresh coriander
  leaves and stalks, finely chopped
8 tbsp sunflower oil
350ml water
  or as required
4 medium eggs
  hard-boiled
6 cloves of garlic
  finely chopped
15g ginger
  finely chopped
8 medium tomatoes
  finely chopped
4 medium potatoes
  peeled, cut into quarters and left in a
  bowl of cold water
125g Greek yoghurt

Optional
For colouring,
not spice

1. Start by making your koftas. Split your onions into thirds, set aside 2/3 of the onions for the sauce. Squeeze the remaining 1/3 in your hands or a cotton cloth to remove any excess water.

2. In a large bowl, add the mince, squeezed onions, half of the salt, half of each of the spices, gram flour, butter and half of the fresh coriander.

3. Mix together using your hands until the ingredients start to bind.

4. In a small bowl, add 8 tbsp of water and 1 tsp of the sunflower oil.

5. Dip your hands in this oily water to coat them. Then take out enough mixture to roll into a large ball the size of your palm. Continue until you have four balls, using all of the mixture. If there's leftover mince, you can use it to roll into small balls.

6. Flatten the four large balls, one at a time, by placing them in your palm and squashing with your other hand until each is roughly 1 cm thick.

7. Place one of the boiled eggs in the centre of the mixture and wrap the mince around it to make a firm ball. Continue to do this for all the eggs. Set aside in the fridge while you make the sauce.

8. Now to make the sauce. With a pestle and mortar, grind the garlic and ginger with two tbsp water to create a paste.

9. Heat 7 tbsp oil in a medium-large cooking pan for which you have a lid, over a medium flame. Once hot, fry the rest of the onions, stirring often so they don't catch, until they cook and darken, roughly 5-7 minutes.

10. Add in the ginger and garlic paste and the chopped tomatoes and give it a stir for 2-3 minutes.

11. Add 200ml water and stir. Put the lid on and cook on low flame for 5-10 minutes. Continue to check and stir throughout—it should become a thick sauce.

12. Now add all the remaining salt and dry spices and stir them in for 5 minutes.

13. Using a hand blender or electric blender, blend the sauce until smooth.

14. Take the potatoes out of the water and add to the sauce, stir to mix. Add another 100ml of water and the yoghurt, mix and then replace the lid. Cook for 10 minutes.

15. Now, place the koftas carefully on top of the sauce one at a time (do not mix in). Cook on a medium flame with the lid on for 15 minutes.

Do not stir

16. Take the lid off and carefully flip the koftas over (again, do not mix in). Reduce the heat to low and cook for a further 15 minutes until the meat is cooked.

17. Check the potatoes are cooked through using a knife or fork to pierce. Turn off the heat.

18. Carefully scoop out the large koftas with a slotted spoon and place them on a plate. Cut each kofta in half.

19. Pour the sauce and potatoes into bowls and place the two halves of koftas in each with the egg side facing up. Garnish with freshly chopped coriander.

"Suji ka Halwa, by my mama."

"Biryani, also by my mama."

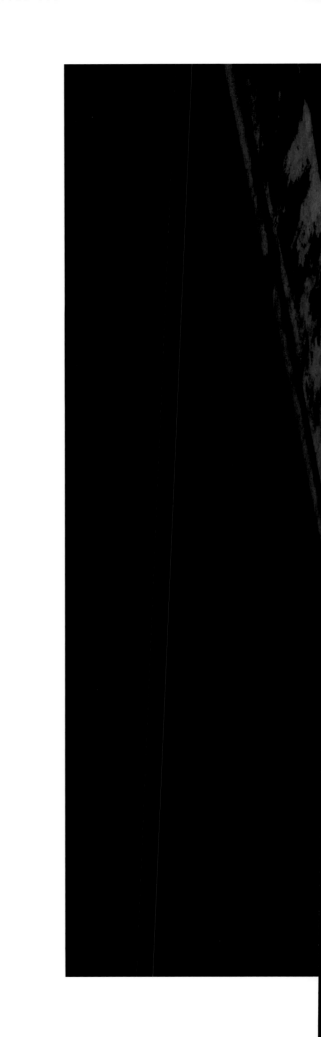

"My mum would cook saucy aloo curry.
Since she passed, my wife makes it for me."

MURGH MAKHANI (GF)

↗ This is my top selling dish at markets

A rich and creamy butter chicken curry, originated across the border from Lahore in Amritsar, India. This dish is best prepared the night before to intensify the flavours.

Serves 4-6
Contains nuts

8 cloves of garlic
  chopped
6g ginger
  grated
1 tbsp water
  or as required
1½ tsp salt
3 tbsp Greek yoghurt
1½ tsp red chilli powder
1kg skinless chicken thighs
  bones removed
8 tbsp vegetable oil
2 medium brown onions
  finely chopped
1 tsp garam masala
1 tsp turmeric powder
6 green cardamom pods
2 cinnamon sticks
  broken into small pieces
15-20 raw unsalted cashew nuts
500ml chicken stock
6-8 medium tomatoes
  finely chopped
5 whole cloves
25g butter
100ml double cream
3 tbsp fenugreek leaves

1. Add the ginger, garlic, two tbsp water and ½ tsp of the salt to a pestle and mortar and grind to make a paste.

2. Transfer half of the paste into a large bowl and add the yoghurt, 1 tsp chilli powder and the remaining 1 tsp of salt. Mix together.

3. Trim the fat from the chicken thighs and cut each into 2-3 pieces. Add to the bowl of ingredients.

4. In the bowl, mix the chicken and yoghurt with your hands so it is completely coated. Then, cover the bowl with cling film and leave it in the fridge to marinate for 2-4 hours. ⤷ or overnight

5. Once 2-4 hours have passed, preheat the oven to 200°C fan.

6. Remove the chicken from the fridge. Line a large baking tray with foil and spread the chicken to cover the whole tray. Drizzle 3-4 tbsp of vegetable oil over the chicken and cook on the top shelf of the oven for 30 minutes.

7. Meanwhile, heat 3-4 tbsp vegetable oil in a wide pan. Once hot, add the chopped onions and sauté.

Until turns brown (5-7 mins) ↖

8. Add the garam masala, turmeric, cardamom, ½ tsp chilli powder, cinnamon sticks, cashew nuts, and the remaining half of the ginger and garlic paste. Cook for a few minutes.

9. Add the chicken stock and the chopped tomatoes to the pan and cook on a low heat for 5 minutes while stirring.

10. Add the cloves and cook for another 5 minutes. Turn the heat off and rest.

11. Once the sauce has cooled, purée it in a blender until smooth.

12. Return the blended sauce back to the pan on a low-medium heat and mix in the butter and cream.

13. Add your cooked chicken to the pan and mix on very low heat for 10 minutes.

14. Throw in the fenugreek leaves, stir, cover with a lid and simmer again for 5 minutes before turning the heat off.

15. Enjoy with chapati or pilau rice.

We played cricket with tennis balls wrapped in electrical tape.

MUTTON CHOPS CURRY (GF)

Tender pieces of mutton in an aromatic, creamy and spicy sauce. This dish is best prepared the night before to enrich the mutton chops with the spice flavours.

Serves 4-6

1kg mutton chops
8 cloves of garlic
   finely chopped
6g ginger
   finely chopped
250g plain yoghurt
1 tsp Kashmiri chilli powder
1½ tsp chilli powder
2 tsp garam masala
1½ tsp ground coriander
2 tsp chaat masala
½ tsp ground turmeric
2 whole black cardamom pods
4 whole cloves
1 stick of cinnamon
   broken in half
½ tsp ground black pepper
1½ tsp salt
   or to taste
1 lemon juiced
125ml sunflower or vegetable oil
3 medium brown onions
   finely chopped
8 medium tomatoes
   finely chopped
300ml water
30g fresh coriander
   washed and soaked in a bowl of water
30g fresh mint
   washed and soaked in a bowl of water
2 green chillies
   scored

↘ 1.5 inch

1. To begin, trim the mutton chops and take off any fat where necessary. Then wash them under running water with your hands, so all the blood is removed and the water runs clear. Leave in a bowl of cold water and set aside.

2. With a pestle and mortar, grind the garlic and ginger with 2 tbsp water to create a paste.

3. In a mixing bowl add the yoghurt, all the dry spices and salt, and mix with a fork to combine. Then mix in the ginger and garlic paste and the lemon juice.

4. Drain the mutton chops. Using your hands, add the washed chops into the yoghurt bowl, mixing until they are coated. Cover with cling film, or add to a sealed container, and leave to marinate in the fridge for up to 6 hours.
   → *I leave overnight!*

5. Once 6 hours have passed, make the sauce. Using a 30-40cm pan with a lid, heat the oil on a medium heat. When hot, sauté the onions until they soften (around 5-7 minutes).

6. Add the chopped tomatoes and stir for 3-4 minutes before adding 100ml water. Mix the water in and put the lid on. Cook on a low-medium flame for 10 minutes.

7. Check if the tomatoes have softened and give the sauce a good stir on a medium flame for 5 minutes.
   ↳ *"Bhuna" This means a constant stir*

8. Take the marinated chops out of the fridge. Add to the pan, including all the yoghurt mixture, and stir for a good 5 minutes on a medium-high flame. Then add 200ml warm water. Reduce the heat to low and cook with the lid on for 30 minutes.

9. In the meantime, remove the mint and coriander from the water and finely chop.

10. Once 30 minutes have passed, give the mutton chops a good stir. Take one chop out, and pierce a knife in to check it is cooked through. If not, add another 50ml of water and leave for a further 10 minutes.

11. Add the chopped coriander, mint and green chillies. Turn the flame down to a whisper and simmer for a further 10 minutes.

12. Turn off the heat and stir until the coriander and mint are fully combined into the sauce.

13. Enjoy with naan bread or pilau rice.

He only spoke Pashto, a language spoken in the North West of Pakistan.

This was my favourite dish as a teen ager. Aloo gosht is regularly cooked in every Pakistani home. Although my mum was the main cook in our family, my dad always cooked this dish - He was an expert in meat dishes.

I learnt a lot from him by asking questions about his cooking techniques. I would call him from london to learn his recipes.

ALOO GOSHT (GF)

A true comfort dish of Lahore, this curry is made of tender pieces of lamb leg and potatoes in a deeply flavoured thin broth.

Serves 4

6 medium potatoes
  peeled
1kg leg of lamb
  meat off the bone and diced, bone
  chopped into 2-3 pieces
6-8 cloves of garlic
  finely chopped
15g ginger
  finely chopped
4-6 tbsp vegetable or sunflower oil
2 brown onions
  finely sliced
6 medium tomatoes
  finely chopped
1½ tsp red chilli powder
½ tsp ground turmeric
2 tsp ground coriander
1 tsp ground cumin
1 tsp salt
1.2 litres water
10g fresh coriander
  finely chopped
1 tsp garam masala

or as needed

1. Place the peeled potatoes into a bowl of cold water and leave to the side. Wash the chopped lamb and bones under cold running water for a few minutes. Set aside.

2. With a pestle and mortar, grind the garlic and ginger with 2 tbsp water to create a paste.

3. Heat the oil in a deep pan, for which you have a lid, on a medium flame. When hot, add the onions and stir for 5 minutes, before adding the ginger and garlic paste. Fry for 2-3 minutes.

4. Add the chopped tomatoes and stir until softened.

5. Add the salt and all of the spices except the garam masala and stir well, before adding 150ml water. Cook until the sauce thickens.

6. Add the lamb and the bone to the pan and stir on a medium flame for 5 minutes.

7. Stir in 500ml of warm tap water. Put the lid on the pan and cook on a low-medium flame for 30 minutes.

8. Once the lamb is cooked, take the lid off and stir for a few minutes.

9. Take the peeled potatoes out of the cold water and cut them into quarters. Add them to the pan and stir in, before replacing the lid and turning the flame to a medium heat. Cook for 10-12 minutes or until the potatoes have softened. *Use the tip of a knife to check*

10. Turn off the heat and mix in the chopped coriander and garam masala. Leave to rest for 5 minutes before serving with chapati, naan or pilau rice.

"The daal chawal and palak my mum and dad would make together."

It's everyone's favourite, a biryani. I grew up in old Lahore, Krishan Nagar, and fresh markets opened earlier than any other shops. Everytime my mum cooked it, she would give a list of ingredients to my dad first thing in the morning.

All my life, my dad would go to the same butchers, he knew my dad very well. So my dad buys everything on the list in the morning, and gives it to my mum so she can start preparing the chicken biryani. I loved it when my mum cooked biryani.

MUM'S CHICKEN BIRYANI (GF)

A household classic, both in Pakistan and the UK. A layered curried rice and chicken dish that is flavourful and nostalgic.

Serves 4-6

500g chicken breasts
  skinned and cut into medium size
  chunks
500g chicken drumstick legs
  skinned and left on the bone
750g basmati rice
2 medium brown onions
  thinly sliced
6 cloves of garlic
  finely chopped
15g ginger
  finely chopped
3 tbsp lime juice
3 tbsp lemon juice
2 tsp red chilli powder
2 tsp ground coriander
½ tsp ground turmeric
2 tsp salt
2 tsp black cumin seeds
10 whole black peppercorns
5 green cardamom pods
  lightly bruised with a rolling pin
1 stick of cinnamon
6-8 whole cloves
6 tbsp plain yoghurt
8-10 tbsp sunflower oil
  or as required
45g fresh coriander
  washed and finely chopped
6 tbsp mint
  washed and finely chopped
½ tsp yellow food colouring
½ tsp orange food colouring
250ml milk
3 litres water
  or as required

1. With a pestle and mortar, grind the garlic and ginger with 2 tbsp water to create a paste.

2. Heat the milk to be lukewarm, then transfer to two 125ml glasses. In one glass, add the yellow food colouring. In the other glass, add the orange food colouring. Set aside.

3. Combine the chicken pieces in a large bowl with the yoghurt, lime juice, ginger and garlic paste, red chilli powder, ground coriander, turmeric and salt. Mix well with your hands to coat the chicken fully. Leave to marinate for at least 1 hour.
    ↳ 4-6 hours is best

4. Meanwhile, wash the rice and leave it to soak in clean, cold water for 1 hour.

5. Once the chicken is marinated, heat the oil in a large pan on a medium flame. Once hot, add the onions and fry for about 5 minutes, until they have turned golden brown. Set aside a quarter of the onions on a plate lined with kitchen paper to soak up the excess oil.

6. Add the marinated chicken to the pan with all the yoghurt, stir for 5 minutes. Then add 500ml of warm water to the pan and stir for 2 minutes.

7. Add 300ml of warm water to the pan, or enough to cover the chicken, and stir for 2 minutes. Put the lid on and cook for 30 minutes on a low-medium flame, stirring every 10 minutes and adding more water if it's beginning to dry.

8. Once the chicken is cooked halfway through, turn off the heat and add the lemon juice. Place the lid back on the pan and set aside, off the heat.

9. In another large pan for which you have a lid, boil 2 ½ litres of water. Drain the rice and add

to the pan with boiling water. The water should be about 1 inch above the rice, remove or add water as needed.

10. Add the cinnamon, green cardamom, black peppercorns, black cumin seeds and whole cloves.

11. Once the water begins to boil, turn the heat down to a minimum and cook for just 3 minutes. Check the rice is half-cooked by taking a couple of grains from the pan and squeezing them between your fingers. They should feel a bit hard in the middle. Turn off the heat and drain the rice using a sieve. Set aside in a separate bowl to rest until needed.

12. In a new large frying pan, spread half the chicken and sauce to cover the base of the pan, before adding half of the chopped coriander and mint on top. Then spread half of the rice on top.

13. Repeat by adding the second half of the chicken and the second half of the rice. Finally top with the rest of the coriander, mint, 1 tbsp of oil and the fried onions you set aside earlier.

14. Using a fork or skewer, make a few insertions into the rice. Pour the yellow and orange milk mixtures on top of the rice in a circular motion one at a time.

15. Put a kitchen cloth on top of the pan, using the lid to secure it in place. You can fold in the corners so it's not loose.

16. Cook on a high heat for 3-4 minutes. Then turn the heat to a whisper and cook for a further 6-7 minutes. Leave to rest for 10 minutes.

17. Carefully remove the lid and kitchen cloth. Use a large spatula to carefully move the cooked rice and meat from the bottom of the pan to the top on all sides of the pan. Mix very carefully, so you don't break the chicken.

or you can use a small side plate

18. The colourful chicken biryani is ready. Serve with plain yoghurt and my mint, mango and tamarind sauce.

"Mutton korma by mum."

"Chicken biryani by mum."

"Also mum's biriyani."

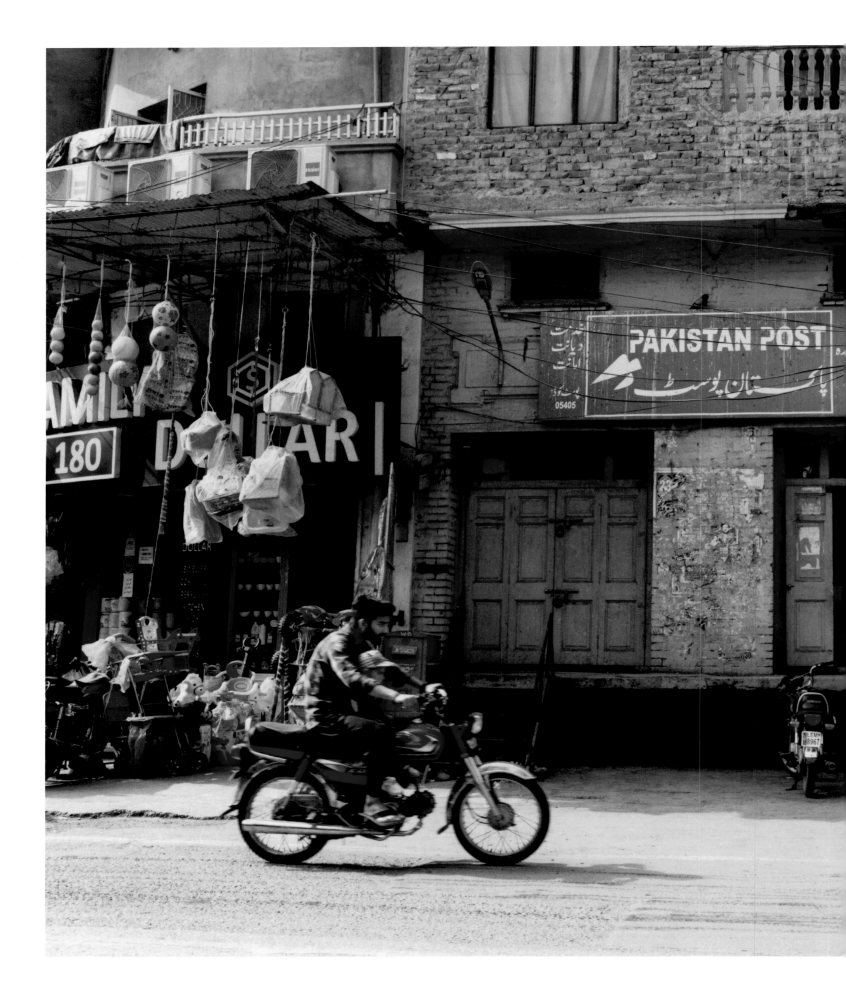

BAINGAN KA BHARTA (V, VGO, GF)

A roasted aubergine mash mixed with tomatoes and spices. Originating from Punjab, this is a traditional side dish in the north of Pakistan and India.

Serves 4

2 cloves of garlic
  chopped
8g of ginger
  chopped
2 aubergines
4 tbsp vegetable or sunflower oil
2 medium brown onions
  finely chopped
3 medium tomatoes
  chopped
1 tsp red chilli powder
1 tsp ground coriander
1 tsp ground cumin
1 tsp cumin seeds
  crushed
½ tsp ground turmeric
1 tsp garam masala
1 tsp salt
2 tbsp water
  or as required
250g plain yoghurt
  or a vegan alternative
2 green chillies
  chopped
20g fresh coriander
  chopped

Be carefull. It will be piping hot.

1. Preheat the oven to 180°C fan.

2. With a pestle and mortar, grind the garlic and ginger with 2 tbsp of water to create a paste.

3. Stab the aubergines all over with a skewer and rub oil all over with extra emphasis on the holes. Season with salt and pepper.

4. Wrap the aubergines in tin foil and cook in the oven for 1 hour.

5. Once cooked, remove the aubergines from the oven and then remove the foil. Once cooled, cut the aubergines in half lengthways.

6. Using a spoon or fork, scoop out the inside of the aubergines and mash them in a bowl, discarding the skin. Set aside.

7. Heat 4 tbsp oil in a large pan over a medium-high heat, then add onions and fry until light brown. Add the garlic and ginger paste and the chopped tomatoes. Stir until the oil separates.

8. Add your red chilli powder, ground coriander, ground cumin, cumin seeds, turmeric, ½ tsp of the garam masala and the salt with a little water. Stir slowly then. Then, once mixed, add the yoghurt.

9. Add the mashed aubergine and stir. Continue to cook on a medium heat for 5 minutes.

10. Add 2 tbsp of water and cook over a low heat with the lid on for 10 minutes, stirring halfway through.

11. Garnish the dish with chopped green chillies, chopped coriander leaves and the other 1/2 tsp garam masala. Enjoy with chapatis.

Mum used to make us cutlets with peas as a snack, at 4:00 pm my dad would say "چائے کا وقت ہے گیا"
It was an after school snack too, we would only be at school 8:00 am to 1:00pm   ↳ Tea time!
because Lahore is so hot in the afternoon.

POTATO CUTLETS (V, VGO)

A warming and filling pan-fried patty made from mashed potato. Mildly spicy, savoury and crispy. This is often served as a tea-time snack, or as a patty for a Pakistani burger.

Serves 6

1 clove of garlic
6g ginger
   finely chopped
½ small green chilli
   finely chopped
2 tbsp water
   or as required
3 medium potatoes
2 tbsp cornflour
½ tsp salt
½ tsp ground black pepper
1 tsp ground coriander
1 tsp ground dried pomegranate seeds
½ tsp chaat masala
½ tsp black cumin seeds
½ tsp red chilli flakes
½ lemon
   juiced
2 medium eggs
   beaten
3 tbsp plain flour
4-6 tbsp vegetable oil
20g fresh coriander

"Anardana" found in South Asian Supermarkets and cash & carry

1. With a pestle and mortar, grind the garlic, ginger and chilli with 2 tbsp water to create a paste.

2. Boil the potatoes fully with the skin on, and then drain. This should take around 10 minutes but keep checking them with a knife. Once cooked, wait until cool enough to handle and then peel the potatoes. *If you have time, leave them in the fridge for an hour!*

3. Once fully cooled, mash with a fork or using your hands.

4. In a large bowl, add the potatoes, cornflour, salt, black pepper, ground coriander, anardana, chaat masala, black cumin seeds, chilli flakes, lemon juice and garlic, ginger and chilli paste. Mix well until combined.

5. Split the mixture into 6 and shape in to flat round circles that mimic a burger with your hands.

6. Dip and coat each cutlet in the beaten eggs and then cover in plain flour. Set aside.

7. Heat the oil in a frying pan on medium flame. Once hot, add 3 potato cutlets at a time, fry until golden on both sides, flipping halfway. This takes around 4-5 minutes on each side.

8. Garnish with fresh coriander. You can have this with chutney, or as a Pakistani-style burger.

To make vegan, use 1 tbsp of plain flour with 4 tbs of water to make a paste

Mum made cauliflower all the time, but without the poppy seeds.
We would have plain rice with every dinner dish, and i didn't
like it, So my mum made me chapati with my Cauliflower.

BHUNA GOBI (VG, GF)

Fried cauliflower encrusted with white poppy seeds. This vegan recipe is full of flavour and is originally known as a winter dish.

Serves 4-6

1 tsp salt
1 tsp granulated white sugar
½ tsp ground turmeric
3 dried hot red chillies
1 tbsp white poppy seeds (or black)
1 tsp brown mustard seeds
½ tsp onion seeds → "Kalonji"
10 tbsp water
6-8 tbsp vegetable oil
1 medium cauliflower
   washed and cut into medium chunks
1 medium brown onion
   finely chopped
3-4 dried bay leaves
3 medium tomatoes
   finely chopped
10g fresh coriander

These can both be found in South Asian Supermarkets

1. Rub the salt, sugar and turmeric all over the cauliflower pieces and set aside for 30 minutes.

2. Using a grinder or a pestle and mortar, make a spice paste with the dried hot red chillies, white poppy seeds, mustard seeds, onion seeds, and 4-5 tbsp water.

3. Heat the oil in a non-stick medium-sized pan on a medium flame. Once hot, add cauliflower and fry for 10-12 minutes.

4. Remove the cauliflower from the oil with a slotted spoon, leaving as much oil behind as possible and leave to rest on a plate lined with kitchen towel.
   → whilst still hot

5. Using the same oil, add the onion and fry until golden (around 5-7 minutes). Now, add the bay leaves and the spice paste, stirring for 2-3 minutes before adding the tomatoes with a dash of water. Cover the pan with the lid and cook for around 5 minutes on a low-medium heat.

6. Return the fried cauliflower to the pan, add a dash of water and stir to coat the cauliflower in the sauce. Bring to a boil, and cover to cook on a low heat for 20 minutes.

7. Once cooked through, turn off the heat and scatter the chopped coriander on top. Mix gently.

8. Enjoy with dal and rice.

"Beef nihari with naan by mum."

CHANA PALAK (V, VGO, GF)

Tender chickpeas and spinach in a creamy and spiced tomato onion sauce. This curry is a classic vegetarian main that is quick and easy to make.

Serves 4

12g ginger
  chopped
6 tbsp sunflower or rapeseed oil
1 medium onion
  finely chopped
4 cloves of garlic
  finely chopped
2 medium tomatoes
  finely chopped
100ml water
  or as needed
1½ tsp chilli powder
1 tsp Kashmiri chilli powder
½ tsp ground turmeric
1½ tsp ground coriander
½ tsp ground cumin
1600g (4 cans) chickpeas
  undrained
500g spinach
  washed and very finely chopped
3 tbsp plain yoghurt
  or a vegan alternative
2 tbsp dried fenugreek leaves ↓ *"Methi" leaves*
½ tsp salt
  to taste

1. Grind the ginger in a pestle and mortar with 2 tbsp water to make a paste and set aside.

2. Heat the oil on a medium flame in a medium-sized pan for which you have a lid.

3. When the oil is hot, add the onion and sauté for 5-7 minutes or until they darken, then add the chopped garlic and crushed ginger paste and stir for 2-3 minutes.

4. Add the chopped tomatoes and 100ml tap water and mix well.

5. Add all of the dry spices, except the fenugreek leaves. Mix well, adding a little more water if the sauce is too dry. Cover with the lid and cook on a medium flame for 5 minutes or until all the tomatoes are softened.

6. Add the chickpeas including the water from half of the cans. Stir to mix for 2-3 minutes before replacing the lid and cooking on a low heat for 20 minutes.

7. Then take around a quarter of the chickpeas from the pan into a bowl and mash them with a fork before returning them to the pan.

8. Add the finely chopped spinach and yoghurt to the pan and mix. Cook for 5-7 minutes, stirring throughout while checking it's not too watery or dry and adjusting where needed.

There should be enough water to cook the spinach ↗

9. Add the fenugreek leaves and stir. Turn the heat down to a whisper and cook for 5 minutes with the lid on.

10. Add salt to taste. Enjoy with pilau rice or chapati.

SERFRAZ FRIES (VG)

A Pakistani twist on homemade french fries. These masala fries are tossed in a spice blend and are often sold in street markets.

Serves 4

500g large potatoes
    skin on, washed and sliced into chips
1 tbsp cornflour
125g plain flour
¼ tsp red chilli powder
1 tsp mango powder
2 tsp chaat masala
¼ tsp garam masala
2 tsp cumin seeds
    dry roasted and crushed
2 tsp coriander seeds
    dry roasted and crushed
¼ tsp black salt
250ml sunflower or vegetable oil
½ green pepper
    sliced thinly
15g fresh coriander
    chopped
1 tsp salt
    or to taste

"Amchoor" from South Asian Supermarkets!

1. Soak the potatoes in a bowl of cold water for 5 minutes, before taking them out and putting them on a large plate. Dry with a kitchen towel. *Paper or cloth towel!*

2. In a bowl, add the cornflour, plain flour and half of the spices. Mix in the potatoes with your hands and make sure they are fully coated.

3. Heat the oil on a medium-high heat and fry the potatoes for 5 minutes until they are half-cooked through. Set aside on a plate lined with kitchen towel.

4. In a separate frying pan, heat 3 tbsp of oil on a medium heat. Once hot, add the green peppers and fry for 4-5 minutes.

5. Now add the fried chips into the pan with the peppers and sprinkle the remainder of the dry spices on top. Stir until all the chips are coated and fry for 5-7 minutes until cooked through.

6. Sprinkle with coriander to garnish, and salt to taste.

You might need to do this in a few batches!

"My mum's aloo paratha with tamarind chutney."

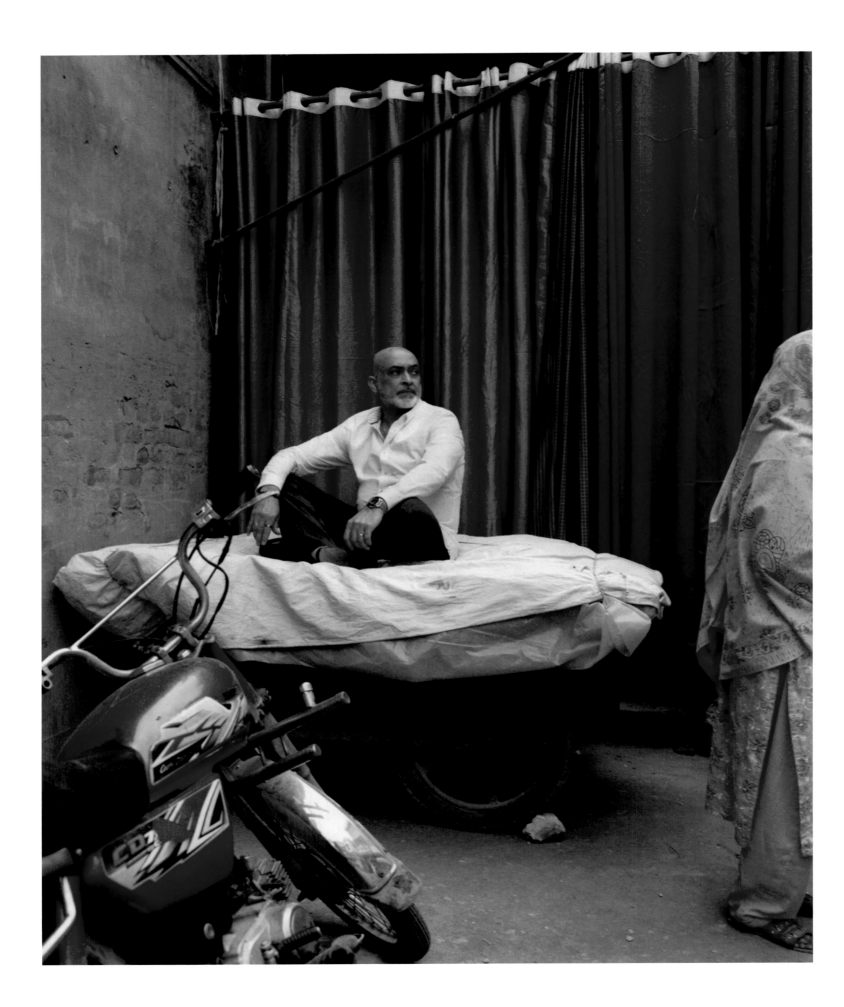

PILAU RICE (VG, GF)

Pilau is a fluffy and fragrant rice dish, infused with a variety of spices. You can find a different version of this dish in every Pakistani household.

Serves 4-6

500g basmati rice
  rinsed under running water
6 tbsp vegetable or sunflower oil
1 medium onion
  finely sliced
1 clove of garlic
  finely chopped
2 tsp cumin seeds
1 tsp onion seeds
1 tsp ground coriander
2 tsp garam masala
6 whole cloves
10 whole peppercorns
1 tsp salt
Boiling water
  as required

Approx 1 inch above the rice!

1. Soak the washed rice in a bowl of cold water for 30 minutes.

2. 20 minutes in, heat the oil on a medium heat in a large non-stick pan. Once hot, add the onion and fry until golden, stirring often so they don't catch.

3. Once darkened, add the garlic, cumin seeds, onion seeds, ground coriander, garam masala, cloves, peppercorns and salt. Sauté for 2-3 minutes.

4. Drain the cold water from the rice and add it to the pan. Stir very gently and add enough boiling water to cover the rice comfortably. Cover with the lid and bring to a boil on a medium flame for 10 minutes.

5. After 10 minutes, check if the rice has enough water, then cover the pan with a kitchen cloth and secure it with a lid. Turn the heat down low and simmer for another 10 minutes, until you see the steam coming out of the pan.

6. Once the rice is cooked, leave to rest for 5 minutes before serving.

Serve this with any of my dishes!

"Mum's biryani."

"Also chicken biryani, by my mum."

KACHUMBER SALAD (VG, GF)

A fresh, colourful and vibrant salad with crunchy cucumber and juicy mango. This can be served as main for something lighter, or as a side.

Serves 4

½ large cucumber
   peeled with the seeds scooped out and
   finely diced
1 medium tomato
   seeds removed and then finely diced
4 red radishes
   washed and finely diced
½ red bell pepper
   finely diced
½ green bell pepper
   finely diced
1 jalepeño
   finely diced
½ large mango
   peeled and finely diced
½ large pear
   peeled and finely diced
½ small white cabbage
   finely diced
6 tbsp pomegranate seeds
40g coriander, stalks and leaves
   finely chopped
40g mint
   leaves only, finely chopped
½ tsp black salt
½ tsp salt
1 lemon
   juiced
½ red onion
   thinly sliced and soaked in cold water
   with ¼ tsp salt
2 tsp cumin seeds
   dry roasted
1 tsp chaat masala

1. Throw all the ingredients, except the lemon juice, onions, cumin seeds and chaat masala, into a large mixing bowl. Mix together thoroughly.

2. Remove the red onion from the water and squeeze out any excess liquid before adding it to the bowl.

3. Once the cumin seeds are dry roasted and cooled down, crush them into the bowl using the palms of your hands to grind.

4. Add the lemon juice and chaat masala into the bowl and mix.

5. Serve chilled.

Cut everything very small for the best results!

Ideally leave in the fridge for 1 hour!

"Mum's pilau. Whenever my mum cooks any curry I always ask her to make pilau rice with cumin seeds. I don't go out to restaurants because I love to eat at home with my family."

MINT, MANGO & TAMARIND SAUCE (VG, GF)

A sweet, tangy and spicy sauce that is full to the brim with flavour. This is the perfect accompaniment to our Serfraz pakoras.

Makes 1L

½ large mango
   hard to just ripened
1 tbsp mustard or vegetable oil
650ml water
   or as needed
170g tamarind ready-made sauce
1 clove of garlic
   finely chopped
6g ginger
   finely chopped
60g mint
   leaves only, finely chopped
30g fresh coriander
   leaves and stalks, washed and finely
   chopped
½ red pepper
   deseeded and finely diced
1 tsp chilli powder
1 tsp ground cumin
¼ tsp ground turmeric
½ tsp chaat masala
1 tsp dry mango powder   *"Amchoor"*
½ tsp salt
   or as needed
¼ tsp black salt
½ tsp black pepper powder
1 tbsp granulated white sugar

1. Peel the mango and cut off as much pulp as you can, using a sharp knife. Cut into small chunks keeping the centre to one side.

2. Heat the oil in a deep saucepan for which you have a lid on a low flame. Once hot, add the pieces of mango and the centre stone and stir fry for 2-3 minutes.

3. Add the water to the pan and mix. Put the lid on and cook for 10 minutes on a low-medium heat.

4. Add the ready-made tamarind sauce and the chopped garlic and ginger. Stir in for 1-2 minutes.

5. Add the chopped mint, coriander and red pepper and stir. Cover with the lid and cook on a low-medium flame for a further 10 minutes.

6. Add all the dry spices, salt, pepper and sugar. Mix well, place the lid back on, and cook on a low-medium flame for 10-15 minutes until the sauce thickens and starts to boil.

7. Turn off the heat and allow the mixture to cool for 30 minutes. Remove the mango stone.

8. Once cooled, blend the sauce in batches until smooth. Transfer the smooth sauce to a mixing bowl to cool further.

9. Once at room temperature, add the sauce into bottles or jars and store it in the fridge.

10. Enjoy with pakoras, or as a dip with any meal.

Best Served Chilled

"Peas pilau by mama."

PUDINA & DHANIYA CHUTNEY (VG, GF)

A refreshing coriander and mint sauce that is used as a dip, made with only a handful of ingredients.

Serves 4

½ tsp cumin seeds
2 tbsp chana dal
60g fresh coriander
   leaves and stalks, washed and
   roughly chopped
60g mint
   leaves only, washed and
   roughly chopped
1-2 green chillies
   roughly chopped
5g ginger
   roughly chopped
3 garlic cloves
   roughly chopped
1 lemon
   juiced
½ tsp chaat masala
½ tsp black salt
½ tsp salt
5 tbsp water
   or as required

Depending on how spicy you like it

1. Dry-roast the cumin seeds and chana dal in a dry pan for 2-3 minutes over a medium heat. Set aside to cool for 5 minutes.

2. Add the cumin seeds and chana daal to the grinder, and grind to a powder. *or pestle + mortar!*

3. Add the coriander, mint, green chillies, ginger, garlic, lemon juice, chaat masala, black salt and salt. Press down to the bottom of the grinder with a spoon.

4. Add 2 tbsp water and turn on the grinder for 2-3 minutes. Use a spoon to clear the side and push down again. Add 2 more tbsp of water and repeat until the chutney is smooth and thick—add another tbsp of water if needed and grind again.

5. Transfer into a jar or bowl and cool in the fridge.

In batches if needed

"Dal with roti by mama."

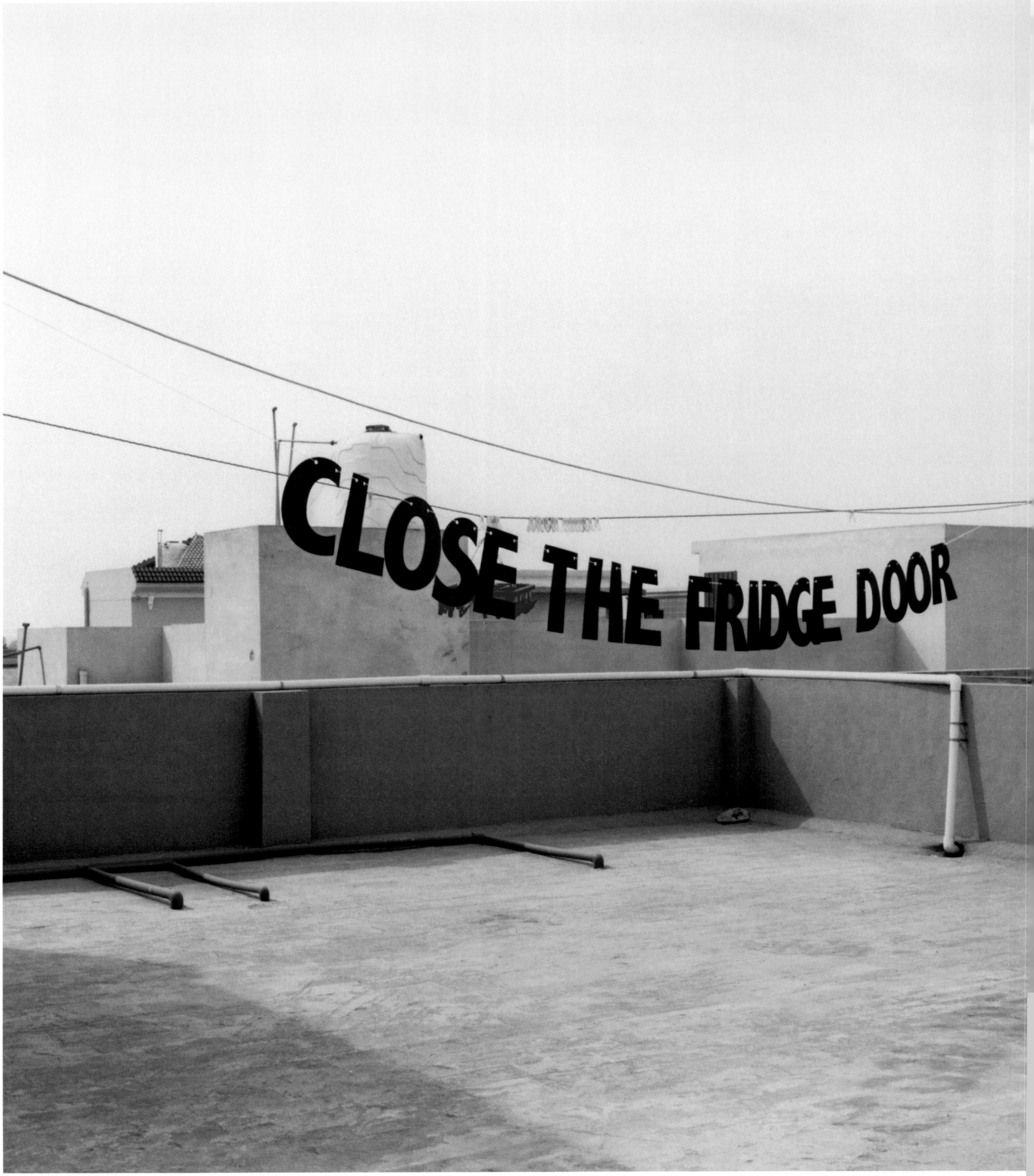
CLOSE THE FRIDGE DOOR

Next to our house in a little alley was a sweet shop, they cooked Gulab Jamuns outside in a large wok. We used to play cricket there too. I'd accidentally hit the tennis ball into the hot oil and it would splatter everywhere – they would be very cross!

It smelt down the street, oily and sweet. I remember watching them make it, putting a wet cloth on top, throwing them into the oil.

GULAB JAMUNS (V)

A dessert made of powdered milk dough balls, soaked in a sweet and rich syrup, topped with a sprinkle of crunch. This dessert takes around 2 hours for the best results.

Serves 6-8 (makes 15-20 jamuns)
Contains nuts

800ml water
200g granulated sugar
⅛ tsp orange food colour powder
3 green cardamom pods
   ground to a powder
2 tsp rose water
1 tsp lemon juice
125g dry milk powder *(I use Nido baby full milk powder)*
2 tbsp (heaped) plain flour
3 tbsp fine semolina
1 tsp baking powder
1 tbsp ghee
   room temperature *(I use Niharti brand, from a South Asian shop)*
1 medium egg
   beaten, room temperature
3 tbsp whole milk
   room temperature
750ml sunflower oil
Shredded coconut
   to garnish
Cake sprinkles
   to garnish
8 pistachio kernels
   roughly chopped, to garnish
} optional

1. Bring 800 ml water to a boil in a medium size pot for which you have a lid.

2. Once it starts to gently bubble, add the sugar and bring to a simmer. Add the food colouring and cardamom powder. Stir into the water, until the sugar is dissolved.

3. On the lowest heat, leave the mixture for 45 minutes with the lid on. The mixture should reduce slightly but still be watery.

4. Once you are happy with the consistency, turn off the heat. Add the rose water and lemon juice to the syrup. Stir to mix in and set aside with the lid on.

5. In a large mixing bowl, make a dough by adding the dry milk powder, plain flour, fine semolina and baking powder. Mix the ingredients together with a spoon.

6. Make a small well in the middle of the dry flour for the ghee. Add ghee and rub in with your fingers to make a crumbly consistency.

7. Then add the beaten egg to the mixture, continue to mix with your hands until the egg is mixed in.

8. Add the room temperature milk to the mixture, 1 tbsp at a time. Mix with your hands until all the milk is in and a smooth ball of dough is formed. You can add another tablespoon of milk if the dough is a little dry, or another tablespoon of semolina if too wet.

9. Cover your hands with oil to remove the dough from the bowl and roll into a neat ball. Cover with cling film so it is airtight, set aside at room temperature for 30 minutes.

10. Once 30 minutes has passed, heat 750ml of oil in a deep wok on a low-medium heat for 5-6 minutes while preparing the jamuns.

11. Grease a large plate with some oil. Take the dough out of the cling film and place on the large plate.

12. Grease your hands with oil again. Roll the dough into separate balls of approximately 3cm diameter.

13. One ball at a time, roll in circular motions between your palms, with a slight squeeze to make them smooth and even. There should be approximately 15-20 jamun dough balls. Place them on the greased plate.

14. The oil in the wok should be approximately 110 degrees when you put the jamun balls in, which is less hot than deep-frying oil, as you don't want the jamuns to brown too quickly. There should be enough oil to fully cover the jamun balls.

15. Gently place half of the balls in the oil. They will drop to the bottom of the wok at first. Leave the temperature on low-medium heat until they rise to the top, which should take around 3-4 minutes.

16. Once all have risen, turn the heat up to medium-high. Now stir the balls in a circular motion, so they cook on all sides until they have darkened to a golden brown all over. The jamuns balls will increase in size during this process.

17. Check the heat of the syrup has settled to around 65 degrees celsius—this is a hot temperature but not boiling hot.

18. Gently take out the balls from the oil with a slotted spoon and place into the pot with the warm syrup. This is with no flame.

19. For the remaining half of the jamun balls, repeat by turning down the heat back to 110 degrees and follow the previous 4 steps.

20. Once all the jamun balls are in the syrup swirl them in the pot every 5 minutes, for a total of 30 minutes. For best results, leave to soak in the syrup for 1-2 hours.

21. Remove from the pot with a slotted spoon and place in a bowl (3 per person). Drizzle extra syrup on top.

22. Enjoy at room temperature or heated up in the microwave for 30 seconds.

23. Finally, sprinkle with the shredded coconut, cake sprinkles and/or pistachio to serve. It can also be served with a scoop of vanilla ice-cream.

It can also be enjoyed straight from the fridge

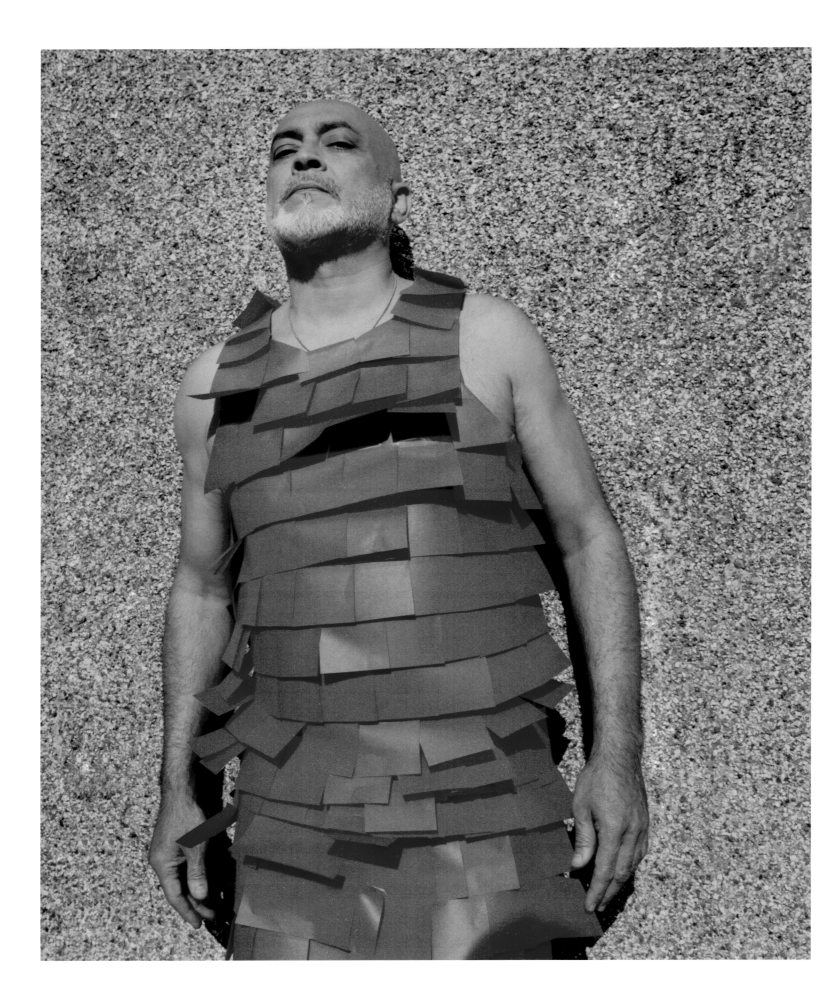

Tami: What is the neurological condition that you have?

Tony: I live with hydrocephalus, which is easiest explained as too much water in the brain. It's an excess of cerebrospinal fluid, too much to be absorbed properly into the bloodstream. It puts pressure on the brain, which for me meant I got blackouts, fainting occasionally and awful headaches all my life.

Tami: What were the blackouts like?

Tony: It would often be when I'm standing up quickly or shake my head too much or sneezing. I used to work as a taxi driver when I first came to England at 19 years old. I often did night shifts taking people to Gatwick airport; sometimes when I sneezed or even just turned my head too quickly to talk to the passengers I would get a blackout. This meant I would literally see black, completely lose my vision. I would try and keep a normal face so the passengers didn't know—it was very scary.

I went to the doctors about it and that's how I found out I had hydrocephalus. I remember I used to take about 10 painkillers a day quite often as a teenager to get rid of my headaches. But I never went to the doctors when I lived in Pakistan, my dad would always just give me home remedies. They say I was born with hydrocephalus and if they had known when I was born, they would have sorted it and I'd never have had these problems.

Tami: Can you explain how you lost your memory?

Tony: The memory loss happened in my mid-20s. The back of my head has been opened in surgeries over 15 times. They would put a tube in to drain the excess water. The accident happened on—I think—the third ventriculostomy. When the surgeons were pulling the camera out of my brain after draining the fluid, they knocked something in my brain which damaged my short term memory. *(Dad cries here.)*

They didn't say "sorry, you're going to have memory loss"—they said something had happened but hopefully everything will be OK. But the recovery from the surgery was bad, I could spend the whole day with someone but after they'd left, I wouldn't remember who I was with, just a faint memory that someone was there. I would cry a lot, thinking what had they done to me, but it got a bit better with time. I had to learn to live with it. I would start using Post-It notes to write on as a way to remember. I still use them: they're stuck on my wallet, on the front door, on the fridge, everywhere. That's what our pictures with the text hanging on string is inspired by these Post-It notes. From "the rice is on the hob" to "close the fridge door", these are reminders that often my wife, Hazel, will write for me so that I don't forget. Sometimes I can forget dangerous things like leaving my keys in the front door or leaving the oven on, so it's important that I have these reminders.

Tami: What was your memory like before the surgery?

Tony: When I was in college, I did maths and was very good at it. I used to literally memorize equations and was very quick at solving mathematical problems. Before mobile phones and everything, I could remember all my friends' and family's phone numbers off by heart. When I met my wife Hazel, in a bar in Richmond back in 1990, she gave me her number but I didn't write it down. Hazel thought I wasn't interested, but I had memorized it in my head. She was so surprised when I called her a few weeks later. Luckily cooking falls into my long term memory, which is still very good, so I use cooking as a therapy a lot of the time. It's something I don't forget because it's in my muscle memory almost.

Tami: You grew up in Lahore, Pakistan until you were 19 years old. How did you make the decision to move to England?

Tony: I was struggling to find work. At the time, I was working for my uncle in his electric parts shop on next-to-nothing per hour. My cousins Naveed and Irfan were in England studying at the time, I used to call them and they'd always tell me I should come to England. So I moved! I stayed with them when I first came to London, in Hounslow. Whenever I opened the fridge, there was nothing in there but eggs. I was always eating eggs and bread, every day.

Tami: Did you feel homesick leaving Pakistan?

Tony: Everything smelt strong in Lahore. The frying onion smell, the smell of throwing spice into hot oil, the smells are everywhere. None of those smells were in London, I missed the food a lot. I didn't know many people either and I didn't have a job at first, so I would spend my time walking up and down Treaty Centre in Hounslow and missing home. Then I managed to get a job in a petrol station, they only paid me £1.50 an hour but I worked from 7am until 11pm so I earned enough money to move into a flat. This flat had a decent kitchen compared to the last, so I had space to cook again. Before that, I'd eat South Asian food from Hounslow Tandoori.

I never really learned to cook when I was growing up. My mum wouldn't let me in the kitchen. Pakistan is backwards that way—men don't have to lift a finger. But I wanted to learn, especially when I came to London and missed the food so much. I'd go and visit my aunty, and she'd teach me in person, and I'd call my mum, she'd teach me on the phone and I'd write down her recipes. Even though my mum was so far away, I still wanted to learn from her rather than cookbooks because these are traditional recipes that have been passed down for generations and that have now been passed down to you and Anusha. It felt good to be cooking food that reminded me of home.

Tami: Do you ever worry that you'll forget recipes?

Tony: Yes! I do worry about this. However, I make sure to write down all of my recipes in notebooks as I'm cooking, so I don't forget any of them. However, as a lot of these dishes are part of my long-term memory from being a child, I still am able to cook from memory.

Tami: What was your home like in Lahore?

Tony: I grew up in the old town of Lahore. In front of our house is a bustling market, with anything you could ever need. In the morning my dad would ask my mum what she'd want to cook that day, and he'd go out and buy all the ingredients from our street, we didn't have a fridge or much storage so we would buy meat and vegetables fresh every day.

   The house was large and old. My dad moved there with his family from India during partition; a Sikh family used to live there. On each floor there are around four rooms and there are four floors. There were probably about 20 people living in the house. There is a courtyard in the centre of the house and the walls of the house surround it all the way round. When you look up you can see a large rectangle of sky.

   The kitchen was very small, no oven or fridge, just two portable gas hobs on the floor and a small work top on the floor also. Mum would sit there, on the floor of the kitchen, and cook for us.

   We had four or five stools in the kitchen—that's where we'd sit and eat our breakfast before going to school. When we ate dinner, we'd sit on a big sheet on the sitting room floor or my parents' bedroom floor.

Tami: Did your mum and dad have different cooking styles?

Tony: My mum and her parents grew up in Lahore and my dad grew up in Ludhiana, India but his mum was from Kashmir. It meant that dad cooked much more spicy food than my mum was used to, the spices were definitely different to Lahori cooking. But I really liked his cooking, he'd mainly cook meals for special occasions, but mum would cook the day-to-day dishes.

Tami: What would you eat when you were sick?

Tony: My dad would make me turmeric water: he'd boil it with turmeric and honey, then cool it before I drank it. My mum would make me Khichri: it's a dish with soft rice and split green lentils that's easy on the stomach. She'd put fresh chicken stock in there as well to give me energy. My dad never took us to any doctor all of our lives, he knew all the natural remedies.

Tami: What would you eat in the restaurant as a treat?

Tony: Karahi gosht with chicken. I have a friend, Faheem, who is three years older than me. We would go with a group of friends to a restaurant as a treat. You would choose your chicken outside the restaurant! They would kill and cook it all fresh. They weigh it alive, you choose your spices and everything, then 40 minutes later you get that chicken as a dinner.

Tami: What was your favorite street food in Lahore?

Tony: We didn't have much money, so we didn't go to restaurants often, but if we ate out it would be street food. They had everything on our street—there's haleem, nihari, even egg burger patties now. In the old city of Lahore, in a place called Bhatti Gate with markets, there was a man who used to make nihari. It's a winter dish, with beef and a sauce. You could hardly fit 10 people in his restaurant but he had a pan the size of a big round table, and it was buried in the ground with a wood fire. His nihari would take about eight hours to cook, so he would start cooking at midnight and by 7am there would be about 50 people in the queue already to get his food. All the food would be gone by 8am. Now this man has five different restaurants in Lahore.

Tami: What are the most vivid tastes you'll never forget from Lahore?

Tony: The tastes I remember the most from Lahore are the spicy sauces, especially from a nihari. Because of the flour added to it, it's nice and thick and not too runny. The other taste I can't forget are gajrela puddings—it's a very bitty dessert because of the carrots and almonds. In general, the tastes that I can't forget are the spices and meat from the markets! The food is always so fresh.

Tami: What does it mean for you to cook for people, and to share your recipes?

Tony: I feel so happy to have my recipes published in this book—at the moment they're in hundreds of places and books that I always lose or forget where they are. To have my food living permanently within this book, and for others to see, make and eat, makes me feel like they'll never be forgotten.

THE RICE IS ON THE HOB
TONY & TAMI AFTAB

Thank you above all to my dad, Tony, for being an inspiration to me both as a father and a muse. The last five years of photographing together have been so special, watching your confidence grow and sharing these experiences. I've learnt so much about you—and about myself—through this journey and I hope we can continue to capture our relationship for many more years to come.

To my wonderful mum, Hazel, and sister, Anusha, for supporting my image making and dad's kitchen journeys, neither of which would have been possible without you both.

Thank you to Tom Booth Woodger for believing in and caring about this project since day one, and for being the brains behind this book. This project couldn't have happened without you, so thank you for all your time, skill and friendship.

Thank you to the team behind WeTransfer for having trust and care the whole way through the project, and for giving us the support to make this book come to life; Suzanne Tromp, Faye Quinn, Danielle Boelling, Hannah Ewens, Liv Siddall, Polly Bussell and Holly Fraser.

Finally, thank you to Jyoti Patel, Phoebe Somerfield, Chan Photographic, Kay Kimura Dickinson, Ruby Boddington, Jamie Allen Shaw, Patrick Thomas, Subhan & Roshaan & Goshi & Sehar Ali, Romana Aftab, Shiza & Mohammad Bhatti, Mahrukh Khan and to all my friends who have supported Serfraz Kitchen over the years by eating and working at our kitchen takeovers, and for testing the recipes from this book at home.

TONY AFTAB runs Serfraz Kitchen, a Pakistani family kitchen founded in 2018. At the same time we started collaborating on images together with our ongoing project, *The Dog's in the Car*. Follow *@serfrazkitchen* on Instagram to find images of the recipes from this book, and to keep updated on any events.

Thank you WeTransfer!

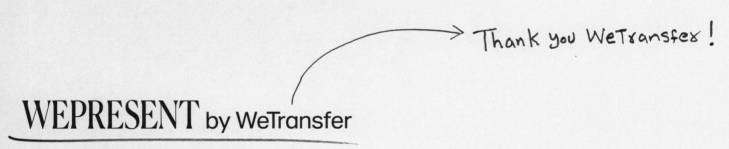

WEPRESENT by WeTransfer

A portion of the proceeds from this book will be donated to Muslim Hands, to rebuild homes for people that were left homeless as a result of the Pakistan floods, in September 2022. 33 million people were affected by the floods, displacing at least eight million people, and placing nine million people at risk of being pushed into poverty. Human Rights Watch have stated that the floods in Pakistan show a direct need for climate action.

In 2020 WePresent commissioned Tami to create *The Children of the Wildflower*, a project documenting a personal journey to Ireland to retrace her grandmother's footsteps. In 2023, WePresent collaborated once more with Tami, commissioning *The Rice is on the Hob*, a project created with and about her father, Tony, inspired by the impact an operation had on his memory almost 30 years ago.

Designer: Tom Booth Woodger
Colourist: Phoebe Somerfield
Printed in Istanbul by MAS Matbaa

ISBN: 978-1-3999-6210-0
Font: Skolar
Paper: Wibalin Natural Olive, Munken Pure 120 gsm & GardaPat 13 Kiara 135 gsm

آپ یہاں نسخہ استعمال کر سکتے ہیں!

You can store the recipes here!